SIX YEARS
IN A COUNTRY TOWN

Pages from
R.F. Leslie's *Charlbury News*

edited by
Edward Fenton

THE CHARLBURY PRESS
OXFORDSHIRE

ISBN 0 9546342 1 7

A catalogue record for this book is available from the British Library

This selection first published by the Charlbury Press, September 2004

© Frances Leslie, Edward Fenton and the Estate of Robert Leslie, 2004

The moral rights of the authors and editor have been asserted

All rights reserved. No part of this publication may be reproduced, copied or transmitted in any way or in any form without the publisher's prior consent in writing

We are grateful to the Senecio Press, Charlbury, for scanning the cover illustration

Printed in the United Kingdom by the Alden Press. This publication is printed on acid-free paper

The Charlbury Press, Orchard Piece, Crawborough, Charlbury, Oxfordshire OX7 3TX, UK

The Charlbury Press is an imprint of Day Books
www.day-books.com

Six Years in a Country Town is a quirky and affectionate evocation of a small community on the edge of the Cotswolds at the end of the 20th century.

Professor Robert Leslie, who wrote and edited the local newsletter in the Oxfordshire town of Charlbury, had a highly individual idea of what constituted news. Through his eyes we see a community in which everyone seems concerned about each other's welfare, and where the only thing lacking is a good local limerick. . . . Yet there is also a darker side, with the recurring problems of vandalism and petty crime (generally blamed on organized gangs from the outlying villages) and above all the worrying decline in the number of local pubs.

CONTENTS

	page
Introduction	7
No. 1, September 1990	13
No. 2, December 1990	20
No. 3, Spring 1991	21
No. 4, Midsummer 1991	27
No. 6, Autumn 1991	33
No. 7, December 1991	36
No. 8, 29 February 1992	39
No. 9, Midsummer 1992	42
No. 10, September 1992	49
No. 11, Winter 1992	56
No. 12, Spring 1993	61
No. 13, Summer 1993	66
No. 14, September 1993	68
No. 15, December 1993	72
No. 16, Spring 1994	77

No. 17, Midsummer 1994	80
No. 18, Autumn 1994	89
No. 19, Christmas 1994	90
No. 20, Spring 1995	95
No. 21, Summer 1995	100
No. 22, December 1995	102
No. 23, March 1996	106
No. 24, Summer 1996	107
No. 25, Winter 1996	109

INTRODUCTION

IN 1972, MY PARENTS Robert and Margery Leslie bought a derelict house in the small Oxfordshire town of Charlbury, intending to move there permanently once they had retired. Even as weekend residents, renovating the house in their spare time, they immersed themselves in Charlbury life. Eleven years later Robert retired as Head of History at Queen Mary College London, and Margery gave up her post as Principal of the Richmond Adult College.

Once settled in Charlbury, Margery became a parish councillor and Robert began to speculate as to how he could occupy his hours apart from walking the dog and frequenting the local hostelries. Over the years, he had struck up a friendship with Father Robert Bulbeck, the priest at St Teresa's in Charlbury. They called themselves Holy Robert and Unholy Robert. When the two Roberts were

Professor Robert Leslie (with notebook) at the Charlbury Playgroup Fair, June 1994: 'It was good to see the Playing Close used for its historic purpose.'

discussing the lack of a local newspaper, Father Bulbeck suggested that my father start one.

My father was a competent typist, so he acquired an Amstrad word-processor and set about learning how to use it. *Charlbury News* was produced by typing up copy, and then cutting up print-outs and pasting them up into pages. My mother would then drive him to a printer's who would produce the newsletters. In the early days my parents would distribute them around the town themselves. They also left bundles of copies at places such as the newsagent's, News & Things, for people to help themselves.

Everything was done in an ad hoc way. Information would arrive as if by magic and, if it did not, Robert would go out to discover what was going on. He would stop people in the street and ask them what they were doing, much to the amusement of visitors passing through, who would sometimes get a mention in the next issue. At the same time he took photographs and filled a ledger-sized album that is now in the Charlbury Museum. Sometimes he would get half a story, and serious errors would creep in, but it was all well meant.

There was never any charge for *Charlbury News* but contributions were requested. These came in with great generosity, sometimes from people overseas who were on the mailing list. My father kept records and said that at least half the cost was met from these donations.

The real driving force behind *Charlbury News*, however, was my mother; and when she became ill, she was no longer able to drive to the printer's or organize distribution. After her death, my father could not be persuaded to continue. *Charlbury News* was replaced by the *Charlbury Chronicle*, the first few issues of which were enlivened by a feature entitled 'Robert Leslie's gossip column'.

What people liked about *Charlbury News* was that they felt they knew everybody and everything mentioned in it. It was like a soap opera but it was expressed in an engaging and strangely old-fashioned tone, reminiscent of the sort of journalism that prevailed in my father's youth. It was also decidedly partial, and it made us all smile.

It is appropriate that this collection from the pages of *Charlbury News* is being produced in aid of the Charlbury Community Centre Appeal. Robert was always an active supporter of local initiatives. He once warned members of the local planning committee that Charlbury was in danger of becoming 'a dormitory town full of retirement homes for solicitors and university professors' if they did not encourage new ventures. He was in a good position to know, being one of that group himself!

He would have thoroughly approved of the prospect of a new Community Centre in the town he loved so much.

FRAN LESLIE

CHARLBURY NEWS

Editorial

Father Robert Bulbeck has a large parish which covers not only Charlbury, but also Stonesfield, Combe, Finstock, Fawler, Enstone, Glympton, Middle Barton, Duns Tew and Steeple Aston. He has complained to me that other places have newsletters which inform local inhabitants of problems and events in their locality, but Charlbury, by far the most important place in his parish, has no newsletter of this kind dealing with everyday problems.

It occurred to me that we might use the occasion of the Charlbury Street Fair on Saturday, 22 September 1990, to publish an experimental newsletter in order to discover the opinion of local citizens on this question.

I am issuing CHARLBURY NEWS on my own initiative as an experiment to test local reaction. If it is favourable, it might be possible to discuss with the Parish Council the question of making this a permanent periodical publication.

ROBERT LESLIE

Top of the tops
Charlbury wins a prize again
WHAT ABOUT NEXT YEAR?

Oxfordshire's BEST KEPT VILLAGE COMPETITION announced that Bloxham had won the Marlborough Trophy for the best large village, but this year the winners' class, reserved for the four winners of last year's competition, was won by Charlbury.

It is to be hoped that this year's award will be received with good grace by those senior citizens who dislike the competition on the grounds that Charlbury is not a village, but a town, having received its charter from Henry III in 1256, if it did not receive one from King Stephen before that.

It is not the designation of the town which ought to worry us, but the problem of litter. The road signs on the outskirts of Charlbury point to TOWN

CENTRE. What the town does lack is the right number of litter bins.

Review of the year

22 September: *The Times* reported that Lord Rotherwick was claiming £1.6 million compensation for having been compelled to give the public access to a path through Cornbury Park.

23 September: The Street Fair was opened by Dame Acne Beverage, a personality who gave some bewilderment to newcomers to the town, but everyone knew that it was Paul Curtis, a member of Charlbury Amateur Dramatic Society.

8 March: Mr Peter Burchett, Chairman of the Gifford Trust, estimated that there would be a delay of two years in developing the old Primary School. Lord Denning has shown an interest in the legal difficulties involved.

18 May: Public notice was given to the presence of 'New Age' travellers encamped on the bridleway near Taston. The Parish Councillors asked Mr Douglas Hurd MP to visit the camp.

30 June: Reported that Mr Douglas Hurd failed to meet Dr Humphrey Juler, Parish and County Councillor, on the site of the New Age travellers' encampment. Mr Hurd went to Enstone Airfield by mistake.

Up to Friday, 24 August: Nothing seemed to happen. We will go to press in the hope that there is nothing to report.

News and views
Fact and fiction

In Charlbury there was once a vicar, the Rev. W.W. Stoddart (1853–1856) who did not enjoy good health. A curate, George J. Davies, managed things very well during his illness, and left behind him a pastoral letter entitled *A Farewell Letter to the Parishioners of Charlbury, Oxon* (London, 1857).

This tract outlined the problems of Charlbury as they existed in those days and many of the problems, if not identical with those of the present time, are not unsimilar.

One point he made was on the subject of drink which was a serious problem in a town which had 'nine public houses to be supported by a population of fifteen hundred persons'. Today Charlbury has a population of over twice that number and only five public houses, *The Bell*, *The Bull* (closed at the time of writing), *The Farmers Arms*, *The Rose & Crown* and *The White Hart*. Not all these public houses open at midday. There is at least a change in that respect.

Davies complained about the love of gossip and those who indulged in it. Perhaps today *CHARLBURY NEWS* can serve a purpose of putting gossip on a scientific and factual basis and inform you of what is going on in the town, without indulging in flights of fancy or speaking with malicious intent.

The Editor of *CHARLBURY NEWS* should be able to help you distinguish between fact and fiction and ensure that a story related at the Co-Op is not changed out of recognition by the time it arrives at the Pharmacy. In that way he may comply with the wishes of the Rev. G.J. Davies.

From cart to juggernaut
Charlbury cannot always move with the times

Many things have happened in Charlbury over the centuries, but we still have a town as it was laid out in the Middle Ages. Thus Hick's Wood has become Hixet Wood, but the street is as narrow as ever and we are now in the age of the motor car and lorry.

As far as traffic is concerned Charlbury cannot move with the times. It therefore follows that the times must spare a few minutes for Charlbury at certain dangerous places in our streets and roads.

* * *

In the old days Waggoner Johnson left Charlbury at 4 a.m. on a Monday morning and arrived at *The Warwick Arms* in Oxford Street, London, on Wednesday at mid-day. If all went well, he was back in Charlbury on Saturday. Before the days of the turnpike roads carts went to Oxford along the Woodstock Way, what is now a lane on the south side of the quarry, and thence by the Ditchley Riding. Happily those days are over.

Editorial problems
Don't shoot the Editor
HE'S DOING HIS BEST

Some people in the town have heard about this plan to publish *CHARLBURY NEWS* and doubtless already have views on what should be its content, but they must first be aware of the practical difficulties that an editor has to face.

The content of a periodical presents difficulties. The views of local contributors may be expressed in such a manner that the Editor will judge it wise not to publish them in their original form. Likewise he may find it necessary to correct a writer's English style. The opportunities for giving offence and irritating people are infinite.

An important question is the style of writing used in articles. It may be asked whether the Editor should follow the example of national newspapers like *THE TIMES* or the *GUARDIAN*, or adopt the methods of the tabloid or more popular press. Should articles be factual and analytical, or may the Editor or writers have recourse to the occasional witticism to make the newsletter more attractive?

In short, the Editor must on the one hand act as a dictator within the limits which he has to set himself, but at the same time be sufficiently democratic to respond to the wishes of the community. His genius for compromise will be taxed by the fact that the editorship involves irritations which will occupy his time and try his patience. It follows that his readers for their part must show him some tolerance.

The White Hart
Over 200 years and still open

The White Hart was one of the nine inns licensed in Charlbury in 1786. A visitor from Germany said he enjoyed drinking in it, because it brought back memories of old times. For the bowls club it is an essential, enabling its members to slake their thirst after the physical and intellectual effort of a game on the adjacent green.

In the summer it was announced that *The White Hart* would be closed from 30 July and reopen on 14 September to allow repairs to be carried out. Thus an unaltered refurbished inn is open for the Charlbury Street Fair. Those of us who may have got the impression that *The White Hart* is closed should walk down Market Street and see for themselves what changes have taken place!

Late news

The Bull had been put up for sale. On the morning of 27 August a notice appeared: 'SOLD subject to contract.' *29 August*: Berry's Nationwide Estate Agents confirm that *The Bull* has NOT been sold. Yobos had altered the notice.

A public servant
Give Ernie his due

Ernie Akers, who mans Charlbury Station, sells newspapers on the system of the passengers taking a paper and putting their money in the box. Some people have been taking their papers without paying for them, in consequence of which in one week in October Ernie lost £10.00.

Obviously no one can afford to sustain losses on this scale. The Editor suggests that those with sympathy for him might brighten his Christmas by adding a little extra money.

Not all the passengers who use Charlbury Station actually live in the town. Readers should draw the attention of such persons to the losses which Ernie has sustained. Will the editors of the *STONESFIELD SLATE*, *ENSTONE ENSIGN*, and the *PARISH MAGAZINE OF CHADLINGTON AND SPELSBURY* please note the contents of this article?

M40 motorway
Does it help us?

On 16 January Malcolm Rifkind opened the last section of the M40, which means that people in Birmingham can travel direct to West London and West Londoners can go direct to Birmingham without having to use the M1 and M6.

We in Charlbury naturally ask what use the M40 can be to us. If readers have any advice on how to get onto the M40 from Charlbury, will they please inform us?

The wrong holes

It is said that the wisest memories we have in old age are the tomfool things we did when we were young. The youth of the town are reminded that the ultimate destination of the golf ball is the hole at the green.

One resident of Enstone Road complains that golf balls have three times broken windows in her house. Young people are therefore asked to remember that the hole in the window is not what they are aiming at. While no one objects to their practising the art of golf on Nine Acres or elsewhere, they should remember that the hole in the window does not exist until they make it.

A hole on a tee costs nothing after it has been made and can be used again and again, but three holes in a window, which must be repaired each time they are made, can be very expensive. Young golfers will appreciate the truth of this when they grow up and have windows of their own.

Shopping in Charlbury
A crucial question we must answer

On Saturday, 8 December 1990, truth came to Charlbury. Snow began to fall and by the end of the day it lay thick on the ground. In these circumstances it was clear that many of our fellow citizens decided that they must do their shopping in Charlbury rather than go elsewhere.

It then became apparent that Charlbury has lost many of its shops in recent years. The situation may be summed up on the day of the snowfall by the remark made by one lady who discovered that all the bread had been sold: '. . . and they haven't even restocked their shelves. I do wish we had done our shopping in Cheltenham yesterday.'

It is quite clear that many people go to neighbouring towns where there are super-markets. If they did their shopping here in our town, then the tradespeople would stock up accordingly, but they cannot be blamed for stocking up normally and then running short of goods when an emergency occurs.

A map of Charlbury
A view of the past and present

The citizens of Charlbury cannot have failed to notice that on sale in the town is a map, entitled *The Parish of Charlbury and local footpaths.*

This map is clearly intended to give walkers an idea of where they can go and to remind them of the historic events which have occurred in the district. In short, it does more than the old witticism that 'Geography is about maps and History is about chaps'. Not only that, it contains information on the ladies of the town. It has already to some extent become a historical relic in the sense that some of the detail relates to AD 1990 and we have already entered AD 1991. Thus mention is made of A. Ambrose (Ironmonger), but A. Ambrose has closed.

This event does not detract from the merit of the map, but enhances our knowledge of the town.

It makes one ask whether it would be a good idea to compose a guide book of Charlbury, giving details of past names. This would give us some idea of the evolution of the town. Once there were nine pubs, and even more pub names. A guide book could bring the past alive for us even if we cannot do the pub crawl.

Latest news

There is a Chinese proverb which says that 'No news is good news'. There was no news at the beginning of March. A number of persons who said they had contributions to make to *CHARLBURY*

News had failed to send their articles. The Editor therefore decided to go to press.

Competition
Charlbury limerick

There is one shortage in Charlbury and that is a limerick. Many towns have limericks. We all know about the Young Lady of Wantage, the Barmaid in Sale and the Curate of Salisbury, but there is no one who achieves such immortality in Charlbury in this manner.

A slight problem does arise in the pronunciation of Charlbury. Is it Charl-bury, or the historic Ceorl-bury? There is of course the rather dull one using the historic pronunciation:

> A dear old lady of Hixet Wood
> Said she would as soon as she could
> Go down to Charlbury
> All round by Cornbury.
> The long walk would do her much good.

This one is much funnier if we add the complementary limerick, of which there are two versions, one rather racier than the other. The Editor is certain that the inhabitants of the town know both!

The Editor therefore suggests that the wits of the town turn their attention to composing a printable limerick for Charlbury, which uses either pronunciation, and which is self-contained in the sense that it needs no further limerick to explain it. Entries should be submitted by the First of April (a suitable date!) A prize of *FIVE POUNDS* is offered for the successful entry. The Editor's decision is final.

Charlbury Street Fair
21 September 1991

CHARLBURY NEWS can give advance information on the Street Fair for 1991 so that readers can make a note in their diaries before the holiday season.

Last year's innovation of the Greasy Pole will reappear, as will the Morris Dancers, Chipping Norton Silver Band, the Masons Apron Clog Dancers and Johnnie Chuckles.

The Barn Dance will be held on Friday 20 September after the Three-legged Race. Tickets must be bought in advance.

The purpose of the Street Fair is to raise funds for the Corner House and the Memorial Hall which are not supported by the rates or community charge. It is therefore suggested that citizens of the town impose upon themselves a Poll Tax and patronize those organizations which through their stalls, sideshows and exhibitions make a contribution to local funds. The people of Charlbury will get more fun out of that than they get from the Poll Tax.

Charlbury News
Editorial note

Readers are reminded that *CHARLBURY NEWS* has its first birthday on the occasion of the Street Fair. It is now getting beyond the experimental stage. Do readers wish it to continue? What ideas have they got for its improvement? What news have *they* got? If they do not wish to write to the Editor, he will be available outside Market House, Church Street (next to the butcher) on the day of the Fair and they can tell him personally.

Charlbury past & present
How much do you know?
THE PLAYING CLOSE

When you walk past the Playing Close you should remember that it was an open space at the disposal of the town in the 15th century at least.

In the first half of the 19th century Sycamore House on the Playing Close, with the house adjacent to it, was a boarding school set up by the Quakers. When you eat a bar of chocolate reflect that some of the Rowntree and Cadbury families were educated there. If you eat a biscuit, remember that it had also a connection with Huntley & Palmer.

But please do not practise archery on the Playing Close as was once the custom. On the south western corner there is a garage, once the home of the fire brigade. Before that it was the lock-up where offenders were lodged overnight before being transferred to the court in Chipping Norton. Archers, alas, can no longer be put in it.

Charlbury—
Town or village?

There was a discussion on *Radio Oxford* recently on whether Charlbury is a town or a village. One person who protested that Charlbury is a town was Bert Shayler, a former Parish Councillor.

Mr Shayler insisted that our football club is called 'Charlbury Town'. *Radio Oxford* seemed to think that a place governed by a Parish Council was a village.

We should perhaps look at Charlbury and ask what it has got. Well, it has a railway station, Post

Office, bank, library and a Memorial Hall. There are four churches and a Friends' Meeting House. We have doctors, dentists, a veterinary surgeon, a chiropodist and other practitioners.

Charlbury has three large factories. There are two publishing firms, two specialist printers, three firms of architects, specialist engineering firms, professional geologists, Bartington Instruments, garages, car repair works and other useful establishments. There are numerous firms of contractors and builders. There has been a decline in our retail shops in recent years, but Charlbury is still important enough for outsiders to come into it to do their shopping.

In short, Charlbury is not a sleepy hamlet, but a place of some distinction. One famous inhabitant was Harry Pickup, who took the first three letters of his first name and the first three of his surname and invented *Harpic*. Perhaps *Radio Oxford* might reflect on that fact and ask itself whether it too has gone round the bend.

Snowball at *The Farmers*

We all of us have admired the transformation which has taken place in *The Farmers* in recent years. One of its activities is the weekly Quiz. Mr Harte gives a prize of one gallon of beer to the winner.

In addition to the prize there is a draw. A number is drawn and the competitor who has scored that number gets the prize. If that particular number has not been scored, then the money remains in the bag to accumulate. This is the Snowball.

Recently £25 accumulated and there was a discussion on what should be done with the money. One suggestion was that it should be donated to a local good cause. The good cause selected was *CHARLBURY NEWS*.

The aim of *CHARLBURY NEWS* is to acquaint the town with news and views in the district. One piece of news is that *The Farmers* is a good place to visit and the Editor lures his wife there when he thinks she has done more than enough cooking and needs a rest from the stove.

In thanking Mr Harte the Editor recommends that his readers should go to *The Farmers* and see things for themselves.

Competition
Postponement of date of submission
CHARLBURY LIMERICK

One of the difficulties in composing a limerick about Charlbury is finding a word which rhymes with Charlbury, whether pronounced Charl-bury or Ceorl-bury. A certain assonance can be achieved using the historic pronunciation as in the following submission:

> There was a young lady of Charlbury,
> Who went to make love to a call-boy

We will agree that it is sad to relate she was ten minutes late, but a true rhyme was not achieved. We therefore may be excused from printing the fifth line.

The Editor facetiously set April the First as a deadline for submissions, but on second thoughts he now makes 1 September the final date so that the winning version may be published in the Autumn Edition in time for the Street Fair.

Latest news
Shoes

Malcolm West intends to hold an exhibition of his shoes in the Corner House from 9 a.m. to noon on Saturday, 22 June. Shoes will be available for purchase. The Editor has bought two pairs of Mr West's shoes and says they are very comfortable.

Vandalism

On the night of 31 May/1 June a small car was lifted onto its side in the Spendlove car park. Mr Grant of Longhome, Market Street, wishes to convey his opinion to the perpetrators of this act, which the Editor himself will not repeat.

Finance & production

The Editor wishes to thank all those kind people who have given him contributions towards the costs of production. The last edition consisted of 12 pages, which cost £205.50 to print. At the time of writing the Editor has received £147.70. He has therefore made a loss of over £50.

The people of Charlbury must decide whether they wish him to continue with the production of this local newspaper. It is not only a question of the filthy, but universally desirable lucre which concerns him.

The Editor is in urgent need of help and advice. As he lives next door to the butcher's shop, which is an information centre in itself, perhaps non-vegetarians might inform him of their views on production problems. He will be pleased to accept advice from vegetarians by post or through Gillian Goodgame.

News in brief
Street signs

The signs on our streets need examining. There is the famous sign at the corner of CHURCH STREET with MARKET STREET outside the door of *The Rose & Crown*. It says that the journey to Witney is 8 miles. On the other hand, on the wall at the opposite side of the street is a sign which says that the distance to Witney is 7¼ miles. In addition, the journey to Woodstock is 8 miles, but across the road it is 7 miles. How many old people in Charlbury know, as they have crossed the street there, that they have covered three quarters of a mile or even a mile in less time than an Olympic athlete could do it?

And then there is the celebrated sign for SHEEP STREET. It fell off the wall of *The Bull* some years ago and has never been put back. Where is it?

+ Graffiti +

We are used to the graffiti which the semi-literate youth of Charlbury and elsewhere use to express their feelings about life in general.

The art of scrawling has been taken up by someone with a typewriter. The following message was pasted on the door of our branch of Barclays Bank on 20 July:

> IN MEMORY OF
> THE GOODWILL
> OF
> BARCLAYS BANK
> WHICH WAS LOST FOR EVER
> WHEN THIS BRANCH WAS CLOSED
> AT VERY SHORT NOTICE
> CAUSING INTOLERABLE INCONVENIENCE
> TO THE GOOD PEOPLE
> OF CHARLBURY

The Editor had to explain on 22 July to Mr John Wilson, our Manager, that he was not responsible, though he did agree with the sentiments. The Manager did not disagree either.

Our public houses

British public houses are not dens of iniquity, but places where friends and neighbours can meet in pleasant surroundings and exchange views on the news. The Editor's experience is that some Eastern Europeans think that they would be an excellent item of export to their world, where drinking is more serious and not so conversational.

1 September: LATEST

CHARLBURY NEWS was due to go to press on

2 September. The Editor checked to see if *The White Hart* were open. It was not. There is a shortage of elbow room on the bars in Charlbury. It is very much hoped that this public house will re-open soon.

Limerick competition
Interim report

In Number 4 of *CHARLBURY NEWS* it was announced that the date for submissions to the Charlbury Limerick Competition had been postponed until 1 September owing to the technical difficulty of finding a rhyme for 'Charlbury'.

There have been some submissions which may interest people of the town, but the question arises whether they would interest the people of other towns, and thus secure their admission to standard collections of limericks.

The Editor thinks it wisest in the present circumstances to let the competition stand over until the next edition. He hopes that the examples he has given will spur his readers into action and force them to produce a classic limerick which will give fame to our town for ever! It should not be beyond their ingenuity to bring notoriety upon our town.

Foreigners in Charlbury?

There must be a lot of foreigners in Charlbury at the moment. The Editor has noticed in the early morning when he takes his dog for a walk that they leave their visiting cards about the place on pieces of tin. Some are from Germany like Holstein and Heineken. Some must come from Eire because they are called Guinness and Sharp. Then there is the Australian, Foster. One frequent Italian visitor is Cornetto, but he leaves his name on a piece of paper.

Whatever their nationality, they are clearly of advanced years, because they sit in places adjacent to refuse bins, but cannot walk the 20 yards or so to put their bric-à-brac in them.

Our readers will no doubt think that what the Editor has written is a load of rubbish. They are quite right!

The Sole Trader

Malcolm West, formerly the warden of our Youth Hostel, appeared in business as The Sole Trader, selling his shoes from the back of his station wagon. He proposes to acquire premises in Charlbury, where presumably his customers will be able to see them.

The shoes he sells are very comfortable indeed. The Editor has bought four pairs and finds them most satisfactory.

Bolton's DIY

When asked how he was doing in his shop at Newington House, John Bolton cautiously said that he would let *CHARLBURY NEWS* know at the end of the financial year.

He has an excellent display in his window and the lights are kept on in the early part of the evening for us to see the goods he has for sale. The people of Charlbury are reminded that John Bolton has most things they want and if he has not he will order it.

Karate
A youth activity

There has been a revival of karate in Charlbury. The club was revived in 1991 with Chris Wilson as its overseer.

Karate has five principles: exponents must avoid impetuous and violent behaviour, pay due respect to propriety, show a spirit of perseverance, be faithful and sincere, and seek to develop a perfection of character.

In other words, it is not a violent hobby, but more a way of life.

W.D. Campbell

Bill Campbell of Ticknell Corner, The Slade, had a serious motor car accident in August. He went out shopping in Sheep Street on 9 November. When asked how he was, he said that he was a bit breathless and could not walk far. This has not stopped his producing his weekly comments in the *GUARDIAN* on the subject of Oxfordshire and its wildlife and vegetation, but he does sound breathless. Let us hope that he gets well soon.

Arthur Yerrill

We were all alarmed to hear that Arthur Yerrill, 1 Downsteps, Market Street, had gangrene in his foot, but it is good news to report that he reappeared in Charlbury on 5 November, having had a big toe removed. He has been seen about in the town. It is good to know that he is back.

Editorial

The Editor wishes to thank all those persons who

have given him assistance in this last year. The costs of printing and folding for the last edition were £209.20.

The Editor had received by 14 November £208.91, to which must be added one halfpenny contributed to the Vincent Pharmacy collection box.

A leap forward into the Leap Year?

CHARLBURY NEWS is still in its experimental stage, but the Editor has decided that it will now consist of 16 pages. This is a Leap Year and he is taking a leap forward.

He apologizes to the readers for the mistakes he makes. Sometimes, when he sits at the keyboard, he is weary and ill at ease and his fingers wander idly over the dusty keys. Then his proof-reading is at fault. Criticisms reach him from various sources in the town. One lady has said that she does not want to read it because it does not interest her. Another has said that it is 'a load of rubbish'. On the whole, however, he can take comfort in the fact that monetary contributions towards its production have more or less met his costs. He thanks contributors most gratefully. He thanks also all those who complain that they have not had a copy delivered to their door. That proves that they want to read *Charlbury News*!

Old barn?

There is a house at the bottom of Nine Acres Lane called New Barn. The facilities inside it may be new, but the building was there in the map drawn up in 1761.

A new feature of the building is Mr Sullivan's CHARLBURY TAXIS (tel.: 0608 810501). These taxis *are* new! It is suggested you use them.

Sheep Street

The Chairman of the Parish Council traditionally gives a lunch or reception to members of the Parish Council, with an extension of the invitation to their better halves.

The Editor was invited in his capacity as the better half of his wife who is a Parish Councillor. He felt a bit superior for a change. At the lunch, however, the Chairman, Mr Graeme Widdows, presented him with the sign of SHEEP STREET which disappeared some years ago from the wall of *The Bull*. If anyone should see that Sheep Street has been renamed SHEEP STREET they should thank the

Chairman of the Parish Council and, perhaps, the Editor, who proposes to put the notice back again.

Comment
Apology

The Editor was reprimanded for putting in the last edition details of a well-known Charlburian. He was told to 'mind his own business'. He takes this opportunity to apologize for being concerned about a fellow citizen's welfare. To show his impartiality he will therefore put in some details about himself.

He has to go into hospital on 26 February for an operation, but much will depend upon the report of the cardiologist. In 1979 he was on the operating table, but the operation had to be suspended because his heart was not strong enough to stand the anaesthetic.

He had intended to produce this edition of *CHARLBURY NEWS* in March, but to be on the safe side he is issuing it in February before his operation.

Advertisements

The Editor is asked how much he charges for advertisements. There is no charge. Any activity is treated as an item of news.

Spendlove Centre
Need for a better sign post

The Spendlove Centre plays an important part in our life. Experience shows that, whereas the Spendlove Centre is obvious to everyone by day, it is not always obvious by night.

It would help if there were a better sign pointing to it from the Playing Close side so that strangers coming from outside the town to functions by night could know exactly where it is.

At the moment it seems to the stranger that he is being directed to 'FREE TOILETS'.

Misdeeds

There is not much news to report about wrongdoing in Charlbury.

Vandalism

One annoying activity has been the burning of No Dog-Fouling notices in the town. It is suspected that a member of the younger generation has been committing this nuisance.

Poles visit Charlbury

Charlbury has international connections and this

was revealed once again in May when a party of Poles came to consult with Geoffrey Walton and his colleagues in Market Street.

The Editor went along, to show the Poles that there were people in Charlbury who could speak Polish and were interested in Poland. (The Editor holds the Officer's Cross of the Order of Polonia Restituta.)

One of the Poles said afterwards that the Editor must have been in England a long time because he now spoke Polish with an English accent. It *had* earlier been explained that the Editor was a United Kingdom national, but had once been an officer engaged in repatriating Polish soldiers at the end of the Second World War.

St Mary's Church

Work proceeds in the north aisle of the church. In the course of this work skeletons have been discovered. Canon Martin Chadwick expresses no surprise. He estimates that there have been over a thousand years of burials in the church and churchyard.

Some time ago bones were discovered at The Queen's Own in Church Lane, adjacent to the church. These were carbon-dated at about 800 AD.

These discoveries are a reminder of Charlbury's long history. They remind us also that more contributions are needed for the restoration of the church.

Sheep Street
Sign replaced

When the scaffolding came down from the front of *The Bull* it was possible to rename Sheep Street as SHEEP STREET by replacing the sign which had fallen off the wall some years ago, the Editor having been presented with the missing sign by the Chairman of the Parish Council.

It does however appear that street signs in Charlbury need inspection. The signs are positioned to cope with the problems of the horse-drawn epoch, but do not take account of the one-way system which we now have in the motor age.

The signs should also be repainted. Some local inhabitants say that 'They' ought to do something about it. Who 'They' are is not clear. The Editor, having done a bit of do-it-yourself, would welcome some compensation for the expense he has incurred with the SHEEP STREET sign. Perhaps 'They' would like to give him some money to re-position and paint other signs.

Vandalism on Nine Acres

At some time on 20–21 May the refuse bin holder near the seat at the Play Area was broken up. It was at first thought that this was another act of vandalism, but an eyewitness has said that when the motor mower was cutting the grass it accidentally brushed into the holder and demolished it.

Charlbury diary, AD 1992
Folklore

I asked Mrs Dorothy Lay why her house and shop in Sheep Street was called Newington House. She said that she did not know, because it had always been called Newington House.

These premises as far as I know were occupied in the 18th century by Thomas Gilkes, a clockmaker. I note that Thomas Gilkes married Sarah Fardon of North Newington. Was Newington House so called after her place of origin? Experts had better correct me before I add this to Charlbury folklore.

It is said that Edward Spendlove, a shopkeeper and maltster, died aged 81 years, in what is now called Wallden House next door to Newington House.

Wallden House was once the Post Office, but

the postmaster spelt his name as *Walden*. Perhaps Mr Charles Keighley might like to rename his house.

Illusive news

I never was a journalist, but I now see the difficulties. News is illusive. Captain Charles Denman, RN, of Sheep Street went into the John Radcliffe Hospital. Almost immediately after his wife, Sheila, broke her hip and herself was taken into the John Radcliffe. Then that honorary citizen of Charlbury, Wilf Fowler of Taston, went into the Radcliffe Infirmary.

Colin Brown went to see the Denmans in the John Radcliffe, but the rumour in the bazaars was that the Denmans and Wilf Fowler were now in the hospital at Chipping Norton. This being 1 June, I went round the town to seek the truth.

I got no news I could swear was the absolute truth, but at 1825 hours Judith Hollings called and said that the Denmans were in Chipping Norton. Where's Wilf?

Editorial

This issue is due out before Midsummer's Day. The

Editor has urgent business shortly after that, namely to celebrate his Golden Wedding. In 1942, 164709 Lieutenant R.F. Leslie married Miss Margery Betts BA in Bury St Edmunds. Almost immediately afterwards he was posted to the Middle East, returning for the Second Front in Normandy. Owing to his usual carelessness he was wounded in Germany on 2 April 1945. He did not return to duty till 11 December 1945. His early years of married life were thus complicated. He would be grateful if, in his old age, contributors to *CHARLBURY NEWS* would get their articles in on time and thus not complicate the last years of his life with their procrastination.

Editorship
Time for a change?

CHARLBURY NEWS was first produced at the suggestion of Father Robert Bulbeck. He recently made the suggestion that someone else might take over the editorship. If readers think it would be more democratic to have another editor, he is willing to stand down. The Editor's one qualification is that he lives in Church Street, a source of news.

Art exhibition

The Charlbury Art Group had an exhibition in the Adult Education Centre on 25 and 26 April.

There was an excellent drawing of the head of Mr Walker of Browns Lane. Unfortunately it was labelled 'John'. In fact he is Robert Walker. The Editor thought he ought to Scotch the notion that Mr Walker of Browns Lane is Johnnie Walker. He recommends that anyone who acquires this drawing should correct the title by putting a Black Label over it.

Latest news

3 June: Rubbish made a further appearance today. At the entrance to the Spendlove Centre someone had shredded a copy of the *DAILY EXPRESS*. The Editor had to get a broom and a bucket to collect the pieces of paper disfiguring Charlbury.

0830 hours: Carpets were being delivered at *The Bull*. One more sign that we can live in hope of an early opening.

Wilf Fowler

The Editor made inquiries this morning and obtained confirmation that Wilf Fowler is in the

Chipping Norton Hospital, because someone had been to visit him there. We all wish him well.

Stop press

4 June: 0730 took dog for walk. Discovered fish & chip papers at Spendlove Centre. Decided to go to press. Apologies for all the typing errors and spelling mistakes.

Street Fair
The day of all the year?
WHICH YEAR?

We may say that the Street Fair is the day of all the year, but we must ask ourselves of which year we are thinking. On the occasion of the Street Fair we are looking forward into the future.

Since the last Street Fair in September 1991 the world has been a difficult place and many good causes have been supported by the people of the town. The reconstruction of St Mary's Church still needs our support. There is low-cost housing for which there is a need in the town. The hard-surface appeal needs completion, as we can see when the youth of the town plays football in the Spendlove car park. The problem of the old Primary School playground is not resolved.

A great social occasion like the Street Fair serves as a reminder of our need for unity and to find a solution to our problems.

Editorial mistake
Parish Council meetings

The Editor published meeting dates of the Parish Council in the last issue, but has since been informed by the Parish Clerk, Mr Roger Clarke, that he had got his year wrong.

Certificate of Merit

CHARLBURY NEWS was entered for the Village Ventures Competition of the Oxfordshire Rural Community Council. *CHARLBURY NEWS* was awarded a Certificate of Merit. The Editor does not understand what the standards of the ORCC are, but doubtless some observant watchdog saw the error for which he apologizes above. He was therefore relegated to the Also-rans.

County Council spending
Validity of the questionnaire?

Oxfordshire County Council recently put out a

questionnaire entitled *What do you think about the County Council's spendings?* It said that this was *A survey of opinions in Oxfordshire.* In fact, it was very difficult for those of us who answered the questionnaire to express any opinions at all.

There evidently was no systematic survey of opinion among the population, citizens being able to reply to the questions merely if they happened to obtain a copy of it. Thus you were able to reply if you were only a schoolchild.

Question 4 asked whether the government should allow Oxfordshire County Council to spend more. Question 5 then asked where the extra money was to come from.

POSSIBLE ANSWERS

It seemed to the Editor that no ordinary citizen can answer these questions without a complete knowledge of problems in the county. The ability of a schoolchild being able to give a reasoned answer is small.

There are many problems which we should like to see solved in Charlbury. There is one which concerns us all.

This problem is the decline of our shops. This is due to the fact that the rates charged on small shops are too high. Oxfordshire County Council should get to grips with the real facts.

The Bell
Juan Claramonte

The new licensee of *The Bell* is Juan Claramonte. He is a Spaniard, born in Marbella. He is acclimatized to the extent of his knowing that Charlbury is a town and is pronounced 'Chorlbury'. All the evidence goes to show that he will be a popular citizen of the town.

Barclays Bank
Questionnaire

Some of the townspeople may have had a questionnaire from the Customer Service Centre, Barclays Bank, in Marlow.

It declared that Barclays Bank was always looking for ways to improve service and sometimes asked customers for their views.

This was a long questionnaire on which we had to tick the relevant squares. I found most of it irrelevant.

I rarely visit the Witney branch of Barclays Bank. I do not get personal service from it. It is not like the old days when you could consult the late Cyril Crane, or his successor, John Wilson, at any time. I therefore added a few words recommending

Barclays to set up their branch here in Charlbury again. Charlbury had a bank in the 1840s and still needs one.

I indicated that it was a mistake for Barclays to do a bunk. The name of the Head of Sales & Service was Mike Folly. Wicked thoughts came into my mind, but I refrained from comment.

Charlbury diary, AD 1992
Tittle-tattle

I have been the victim of local tittle-tattle. I received a two-page vituperative letter from a 'lady' castigating me for calling Wychwood Paddocks 'Tarmac Terrace'. She said that as the self-appointed editor of *CHARLBURY NEWS* I should have better taste, etc. etc. You could have knocked me down with a feather. I had never heard Wychwood Paddocks called by that name before!

When the houses on Wychwood Paddocks were being built, a local wag—I know not who—said they looked so bleak that it appeared as if a concentration camp was being erected. He therefore thought he would call the development 'Colditz Crescent'.

My only comment was that once the houses had developed their gardens and vegetation began to appear they would blend with their background. I feel a bit hurt.

Smocks

Mrs Sally Welch of Greenfingers, Sheep Street, gave up being a curator in the Oxfordshire County Museum in Woodstock because of her interest in precious objects of 20th century origin, namely her two children, but she is still engaged in research there as a volunteer.

Her subject of research is smocks in Oxfordshire. She is looking for photographs of men wearing smocks either in this century or the last. Please help her if you can!

Spendlove Social Centre
No sign of cultural revolution

Attention has been drawn in earlier issues to the emergence of the public conveniences at the Spendlove car park as a social centre for the younger generation. Some citizens have expressed concern at this development.

FRESH INCIDENT

Information has been received that a senior citizen of some standing was walking past the Spendlove social centre and noticed that the assembled youths, both male and female, were throwing items of litter about at random. He recommended to them that they should use the litter bins, which are adjacent to their centre, less than a cricket pitch length from where they were seated.

The young people replied in their local patois, which will need translation for those unfamiliar with it. It was first reported to him that they asked him to depart, heterosexually or homosexually, adding that he was born out of wedlock. In fact, their remarks are even more difficult to translate.

Who these people are is difficult to discover. If they are to be judged by the visiting cards which early morning walkers discover, most of them must be called *Benson* or *Hedges*, but it is impossible to discover anyone by those names in Charlbury in the telephone directory.

SOCIAL PROBLEM

This social problem exists. We must ask ourselves if we can solve it. Clearly no answer can be found in treating these young people as mere delinquents. They need some alternative evening amusement.

Premises for an activity might be required. Once *The Royal Oak* in Church Street provided a library and reading room. Behind it was the Town Hall and the YMCA. These organizations no longer exist. *The Bull* no longer provides a pool table. What can be done? Has anyone in the town got any ideas?

Street Fair
Press coverage

The press coverage in the OXFORD MAIL on 21 September was disappointing. It said that the event was in aid of Charlbury Memorial Hall and the 'historic Corner House'. Some will raise their eyebrows at the notion of the Corner House being a 'historic' building. Its front dates from AD 1725.

For central Charlbury it is relatively modern. When Bell Cottage in Church Street began to collapse a few years ago, the surveyors said that the foundations were 15th century in origin.

Literacy in Charlbury
Question of litter

A recent survey of literacy in the United Kingdom showed that many people could not spell common words. The Editor wonders whether in Charlbury we should use the word 'litteracy'. Literacy seems to be very high on Nine Acres, where evidently people can read the warning notices about dogs making a mess. 'Litteracy' abounds elsewhere. There is evidence of dogs fouling the pavements in the town. There are signs also that human beings foul it. Cigarette packets, crisp packets and chewing gum wrappers are more in evidence than dogs' mess.

The Editor broke his record near the public lavatories on 15 November. He picked up two plastic cider containers, three Strong Cider bottles and 15 lager cans. This was in spite of the fact that invaders had reduced the seating accommodation of the area by removing paving stones from the wall. The rumour in the bazaars is that this was done by a gang from Finstock, but of that there is no proof.

Where is Charlbury?
Problem of location and character

As far as ITV is concerned Charlbury is in the South Midlands, but the BBC places the town firmly in the South East.

The Ordnance Survey in its publication *The Cotswolds* (edited by Peter and Helen Titchmarsh) puts Charlbury in the Cotswolds, though years ago Charlbury people used to say 'We don't want nothing to do with them Gloucestershire people!'

The Ordnance Survey describes Charlbury as a

'delightful country town', but makes the comment: 'Despite the presence of many retired people and commuting Oxonians, the town has kept much of its rural flavour, and it has a mouth-watering collection of country inns.'

This comment occurred to the Editor when he went into *The Bell* recently to drink a glass of low-alcohol lager. In the bar were thirteen women and two men. Was this what the Ordnance Survey meant by 'mouth-watering'? He then reflected that as a 'retired' person, presumably disfiguring Charlbury, he should not be a D.O.M.

On p.41 it says also that 'the coming of the railway, which still survives here, has contributed to Charlbury's special charm'. Let us hope that it remains here! Otherwise we will revert to being in our historic position—on the frontiers of Mercia.

Charlbury diary, AD 1992
Ditchley

It is announced that our Prime Minister, Mr John Major, is to hold talks with Chancellor Kohl at Ditchley, which was of course the country headquarters of Winston Churchill during the Second World War. I often wonder whether it was selected for that purpose because it was the-back-end-of-beyond, of which the Germans would not know the existence. It seems that they will know now!

David Halliwell

On 1 November Charlbury received perhaps unrecognized prominence. Our local playwright, David Halliwell, had his play, *Little Malcolm and his Struggle against the Eunuchs*, performed on *Radio 3*. For this play he was proclaimed most promising playwright of 1965. It was said to have 'survived a quarter of a century extremely well'. David Halliwell survives in Charlbury!

Corner House kitchen
International fame

The Rt Hon. Douglas Hurd MP wrote in the *OXFORD TIMES* on 20 September that he had read that £1,000 had been spent on a new floor in the Corner House kitchen 'to comply with European Community regulations'. He checked with West Oxfordshire District Council and was told that in fact it was to comply with 'British Food Hygiene Regulations'. The *OXFORD TIMES* supplemented this letter with an editorial comment on EC food regulations, of which it is not a little critical. The only editorial comment of *CHARLBURY NEWS* is that it is not often that a Charlbury kitchen goes up to the Secretary of State for Foreign Affairs for consideration. The Editor could have supplied the information in Charlbury.

Latest
CENTRAL FREE ADS, Issue No. 001

This publication appeared on Guy Fawkes Day, price 60p. It seems to advertise everything from Cars and Household Utensils to GIRLS!!!

Later still

CENTRAL FREE ADS appeared on 12 November as *INDEPENDENT FREE TRADE*, Issue No. 002. It was stated that 'due to the overwhelming success of our first issue we have changed name'.

Wine tasting

The wine merchants, Telcher Brothers of Southampton, organized a wine tasting at News & Things on 12–13 November in order to promote their sparkling wine, *Veuve du Vernay*, which is available in dry and semi-dry bottles, priced £4.99.

The Editor, officially a teetotaller, tasted it, but his wife, not a teetotaller, asked him to buy her a bottle. Advertising of this kind is a good thing. We hope that Telcher Brothers will come again and put our tastes to the test.

Weigh-in
Sponsored slim
CUTTING THE POLICE DOWN TO SIZE

Our local police are to be commended for their concern for fairness. PC Andy Sharples and PC Ray Hamilton volunteered to take part in a sponsored slim on behalf of the Hard Surface Appeal. They arranged to be weighed in so that there could be no suspicion that they had exaggerated their weight before they began their slimming exercise.

A ceremonial weigh-in took place in the bar at *The Bell* on Monday, 4 January 1993.

It is good to see policemen taking part in the activities of the community. In some countries the police are viewed with suspicion by the general public, whereas in Britain they are fellow citizens like the rest of us.

PUBLICITY

Thanks to Suzanne Huband, our local reporter, the

Hard Surface Appeal received publicity in the *OXFORD MAIL*, the *WITNEY GAZETTE* and the *OXFORD TIMES*. PC Sharples and PC Hamilton got a photograph advertising the amount of weight they had to lose which was 8 inches long, whereas their photograph in the *WITNEY GAZETTE* was only 4½ inches.

More vandalism
Spendlove Centre

On the night of 13–14 February there was further evidence of mindless vandalism at the Spendlove Centre. The For Sale notice on the patch of grass opposite the public lavatory was demolished. It was reported also that four empty bottles, which had contained whisky, gin, brandy and Campari, were found inside the Gents. The supposition is that the sign was wrecked as part of a celebration.

Information reaching the Editor is that the person responsible for these acts is normally a very sensible man who gets out of control under the influence of alcohol. It is hoped that when he is sober he will reflect that the disenchantment with society he feels when drunk is matched by our disenchantment with him when we are sober!

Charlbury diary, AD 1993
Charlbury rumour

I was coming out of the Spendlove Centre one morning and an acquaintance said 'Am I glad to see you! I was told you had died!' How this rumour got round Charlbury I do not know, but one of the purposes of *CHARLBURY NEWS* is to put local gossip on a scientific foundation. It should be noted therefore that, if a clanging noise is heard in Church Street, it is not necessarily R.F. Leslie kicking the bucket. It is normally the sound of a delivery at *The Rose & Crown*.

Hassall Homes

It was proposed to call the estate being constructed by Hassall Homes, off The Slade, Walnut Tree Park, The Walnuts or Nut Close.

To these names the Parish Council objected. Certainly the third of these suggestions might have led to wits of the town saying that it was an area for the mentally retarded. The Council wanted it to be called Ticknell Piece Road. At a meeting of the West Oxfordshire District Council it was decided to call this development Ticknell Piece. This was said by the *OXFORD MAIL* to be 'a battle . . . won by a town council.'

Historical section
Charlbury past and present
CHURCH STREET

In a historical section entitled 'Did you know . . . ?' the *ENSTONE ENSIGN* stated that 'our neighbours in Charlbury, which is now regarded as a town and has an important station, used to have their letters addressed as "Charlbury near Enstone".'

What is said in the *ENSTONE ENSIGN* represents Charlbury as a place of lesser importance than Enstone. In fact Charlbury was a town in the Middle Ages.

In the 11th century Charlbury was said to have been the burial place of St Diuma, the first bishop of the Mercians, an Irishman, who died in AD 658. A charter granted Charlbury a market in AD 1256. Church Street was where the market was held. In the middle of the street was a building called The Shambles, a slaughterhouse. Its former existence accounts for the breadth of Church Street in its centre. There was also a Market House, a market cross, at the top of Church Street, knocked down in 1871. Under it were the stocks, destroyed it is said by a local man who had been put in them when he was drunk and who gave vent to his anger on the following morning by demolishing them with a large stone.

One of the most interesting cottages in Church Street is Royal Oak Cottage. This was a public house. In about 1832 the Temperance Society was established by William Albright (1777–1852). The landlord of *The Royal Oak* tried to organize an Anti-Temperance Society. A demonstration with a band assembled at *The Royal Oak* and marched to the Playing Close where speeches were made in favour of the consumption of beer and porter. In the end the Temperance Society won. In the 1880s *The Royal Oak* was bought and turned into a temperance hotel and reading room. There were other public houses in Charlbury to meet the needs of the Anti-Temperance agitation.

The market no longer exists, but once a year the Street Fair reminds us of what Church Street must have looked like on a market day in the old days.

Latest news

There have been complaints that Margery Leslie is ex-Directory. That is technically true because her number was removed from it by British Telecom in error. She has tried to get it restored. It is 0608 810829.

Man from Mars
Problem of vagrant

At Christmas we were troubled by a man, who was clearly a vagrant. He won our sympathy largely because he appeared at a festive season. When he was asked where he came from he said 'From Mars!' For that reason he became known as THE MAN FROM MARS.

He appeared again at Easter and was clearly not well. He forages in litter bins for food and knocks up local people and demands coffee. He will not accept a can of beer.

It is very worrying when we see a man in poor health and without food. He lay in Church Street for a whole afternoon and did not drink the coffee offered to him, and would not eat.

Lower Watts House
House in Park Street
ENERGY EFFICIENT

The owners of Lower Watts House, a new energy efficient house at the bottom of Park Street, invited friends and neighbours in to see what they had constructed. It is a most splendidly appointed house.

Park Street was very different before the First World War. It contained the Town Hall, the YMCA and YWCA, two fishmonger's shops, a tailor's shop, two dressmakers, a china shop, a large general store adjacent to the churchyard. There was also a smithy. The area in which this new house was built was once Watts Lake.

Double entendre
EDITORIAL ERROR

The Editor in his capacity as a Simple Country Boy from West Oxfordshire did not realize, until his Superior Officer told him, that the name Lower Watts House, which he thought was historically most suitable, meant also that the energy efficiency of the house ensured that it was using fewer watts (electric). Thus there is a double meaning to the name of the house, which must now be incorporated into Charlbury folklore. In short, when we point out the house to visitors, we must smile and tell them with a giggle what the name really means. Energy-saving, however, is more serious than funny-ha-ha. It is a national necessity.

Latest news
Balloon, 6 June

Drinkers at *The Rose & Crown* came out of the bar to look at a balloon in the sky above them. At 2045 hours they were able to point out to Alan Fraser of the Hothouse that he had driven up Sheep Street the wrong way. His error was indicated to him by the Editor, the Chairman of the Parish Council and other councillors. Alan Fraser was clearly shocked by his error. He clearly had had a lapse of memory.

CHARLBURY NEWS
What can it do?

CHARLBURY NEWS came into existence as an experiment. It now appears to be a permanent feature of life in this town.

Its aim is to comment on our life here and arouse discussion. There is a tendency for rumours to start at the Co-Op and become unrecognizable by the time they arrive at the Post Office. This leads to editorial confusion. The town is much bigger than it was and it is essential for those on the outskirts to know exactly what is the truth. The Editor asks forgiveness for his errors.

Seat in Church Street
Now useless

A seat was erected in Church Street next to *The Rose & Crown* for people waiting for buses. We all thought it was put too high up Church Street. Now doves have proved us right. It is covered with bird droppings and no one can sit in it.

Charlbury diary, AD 1993
Charlbury rumour
THE BULL

5 August: One of the purposes of *CHARLBURY NEWS* is to put Charlbury gossip on a scientific foundation. I was called to *The Bull* to hear what Mrs Lucy Wearing wished to tell me. She asked that I put in *CHARLBURY NEWS* the information that *The Bull* was *not* up for sale. Mrs Wearing was not a little indignant at the rumour. Its origin I cannot trace.

Charlbury Survey

I began to think of drawing up a Charlbury Survey. My aim was to deposit it in Charlbury Museum. I learned also that Miss Katie Gadsby of Woodstock Road was intending to do a thesis on Charlbury.

She was thinking in terms of 'rural decline', but I suggested that perhaps what we should be investigating in Charlbury is rural transformation. Certainly Charlbury is a more important place than ever it was a hundred years ago. I had begun to ask people what careers they had followed or were following. My object was only to collect raw material for a survey. One gentleman said 'What's that got to do with you?' and terminated the conversation. I was certainly not trying to be a busybody and ask nosey questions.

In publishing this edition of *CHARLBURY NEWS* I have been anxious to leave a historical record of what the town is like in AD 1993. This may serve as raw material for some future historian writing up the history of this part of Oxfordshire.

Old age
Common disease in Charlbury

One of the problems one often meets in Charlbury in *annodominitis,* a disease from which we all will suffer one day.

I am not suffering from this ailment at the moment, being a young pup of merely 75 years. Nevertheless, I can feel the onset of the problem. I therefore take this opportunity of putting this fact on the grapevine with special reference to HASSALL HOMES, which will soon be in Ticknell Piece, we are told. I should be grateful if someone in this new housing estate would assist me with the distribution of *CHARLBURY NEWS*.

Latest news
Bank Holiday weekend

Unusually quiet in Charlbury with nothing much to report. Most people seemed to be away doing something.

Sunday, 29 August: Nothing much to report except that Alan Fraser and his TJOPS ensemble gave a performance on the riverside lands. This seems to have taken on the appearance of an annual event. Long may it continue!

Tuesday, 31 August: Time for this number of *CHARLBURY NEWS* to be prepared for the press. Necessary to go out in the town to see if there was any more news. As it happened there was no news in Charlbury.

The next edition will be prepared for publication at the beginning of December.

Best wishes for Christmas and the New Year
But it will be awkward!

Christmas and New Year are a time when we enjoy ourselves, buying our relatives and friends presents and receiving them ourselves. This year there is a time problem.

Dates of Christmas

This year Christmas Day falls on a Saturday and Boxing Day on a Sunday, for which reason Monday, 27 December, and Tuesday, 28 December, are public holidays. New Year's Day comes on the following Saturday. In short we are likely to have not a few days of festivity, but a whole week.

Charlbury limerick
Lost cause

The Charlbury limerick has never appeared. The Editor's adoption of the correct philological pronunciation of our town as 'CHORLBURY' has been of no avail.

Perhaps we should concede that Charlbury will not properly be part of a limerick. We can make amends by making a donation to the Oxfordshire Association for the Blind which depends upon charitable gifts.

The Bell Hotel
AA award

The Bell Hotel has been given recognition by the AA in the form of a rosette award for the quality of its cuisine. Out of 4,600 hostelries, only 1,233 qualified for such an honourable mention.

Street marking
Browns Lane

Some time ago Browns Lane was closed for the execution of repairs to the drainage, but the double yellow lines were not repainted. The same goes for the warning signs on the road.

The NO ENTRY sign for cars coming up Church Street now reads 'NO TRY', which we may suppose is intelligible in pidgin English. The STOP sign at the bottom of Browns Lane now reads 'STO'. Perhaps it is just as well that we get few drivers from Eastern Europe, because 'STO' in Slavonic languages means 'one hundred'. Some local drivers, however, seem to want to achieve 100 mph as they fail to stop at the bottom of Browns Lane!

Charlbury's reputation
Good and bad

Two performers at THE HOTHOUSE ARTS CENTRE

said that they enjoyed coming to Charlbury and had been told in advance that their audience would be appreciative, which they found it to be. They came from the north of England.

Whether the town's reputation will be as good in Romania is a different matter. The omnibus, which brought a party of schoolchildren to stay in the Youth Hostel in the summer, was vandalized at the Spendlove Centre when it was parked outside it. Thus our reputation may be good in Northern England, but is it in Eastern Europe? The culprits who commit these acts are evidently not always from Charlbury, but the Charlbury teenagers should not protect them. If these yobos were exposed, the youth of Charlbury would have a better reputation.

Wool shop

The old Wool Shop is now up for sale. It is a very substantial premises, but needs modernization. A rumour in Charlbury is that the nodding Father Christmas which was once on sale there fetched £350 in an auction in Oxford.

Shortage of news

There has not been much news about Charlbury in

our local press. That is not due to the fact that Suzanne Huband of the *Oxford Mail/Witney Gazette* does not visit Charlbury any more for an evening drink, but rather because there is nothing happening in Charlbury which might excite general interest in West Oxfordshire or the county. There are nevertheless social problems which excite interest in the town itself.

It would help a great deal if events could be reported to *Charlbury News* in good time. It should be remembered that it is a quarterly publication and cannot report incidental items of ephemeral interest.

News about people

News about the activities of people in Charlbury is welcome. The Editor will print news which is of interest to the townspeople.

Ticknell Piece

Father Robert Bulbeck, SJ, is preparing a map of the new Hassall Homes on Ticknell Piece, together with the Low Cost Housing Scheme and the plans for the new Bowls Club. He has not yet produced a final version, but it will be most interesting to see what kind of a BOWLS CLUB is proposed. Will it have a bar?

Historical section
Sheep Street
CHANGES OF THE YEARS

Sheep Street is today very much a jigsaw puzzle which is hard to sort out. *The Bull* presents problems. The northern side which contains the restaurant is said to have a 16th century origin. Certainly the window which was revealed on the Browns Lane side during the recent reconstruction is 16th century in origin, but it is clear that the height of the building was raised at some time.

News & Things was a general store established by a Mr Horniblow, son of Dr Francis Horniblow, a Charlbury physician. It is said that he wanted to become a doctor, but did not like the sight of blood. He therefore established a store in which he could sell patent medicines and his business expanded.

The Farmers Arms was once *The Railway Arms*, said to have appeared when the workmen were constructing the railway in the early 1850s. The original plan was for the station to be built at the bottom of Park Street, but this proposal met with objections from the resident of Lee Place. It was therefore built off the Burford Road, but the houses opposite *The Farmers* were not then built and the public house might well have shown the proposed railway station.

Help wanted
Bunting

If we are lucky enough to find an organizer for the Street Fair, we shall also need TWO (or possibly THREE) youngish persons to put up the bunting in the centre of town. John Merriman, who seems to have been coping with this, man and boy, for about 20 years, has announced his retirement.

The chief qualifications are an ability to climb ladders and a good head for heights in a strong wind.

Charlbury diary, AD 1994
Required: thick skin

The editor of a local newsletter requires a very thick skin. It is a pity he is not related to the hippopotamus. Everyone knows that the square on the hippopotamus is equal to the sum of the squares on another two hides. Someone, whose identity must be known to some Charlbury people, composed a leaflet entitled *Not the Charlbury Newsletter* with the headline LEAKED—TOWN PLAN—SHOCK. This was an imaginary article about the proposed redevelopment in Charlbury. Everyone can have his bit of fun, but the copy slipped through my door had the message written on it 'TAKE A HINT PROF! STOP WRITING YOUR CRAP AND WE'LL STOP OURS! A CHORLBURIAN.' This message invited me to think that, if he could call *CHARLBURY NEWS* a four-letter word, I equally could find a four-letter word to describe this gentleman. I remind him of the saying that no gentleman calls another gentleman a gentleman unless that gentleman is not a gentleman.

Correspondence
Shortage

The Editor in the previous edition said that he would save a space in *CHARLBURY NEWS* for persons who had letters about local problems, but he has so far received none.

Mysterious hole

A farm worker from Combe, Gordon Russell, spreading fertilizer on the farm of Lees Rest, was surprised to see in front of him a very large hole. He examined the hole and could not see the bottom. It is 6 feet across and probably up to 100 feet deep. Dr Geoffrey Walton, our local geologist, has offered to examine the hole and give an opinion on its origins. His findings, if he does examine the hole, will be most interesting, because Lees Rest is a residence of 16th century origin.

Historical section
Inns & public houses
WHERE WERE THEY?

Now that *The White Hart* has closed as a public house we must turn our attention to those which existed and have closed in the past. In the 19th century there were nine licensed hostelries open in the town, but there are far more names of inns and alehouses on record. This invites the Editor to invent a quiz and ask where the following places were:

The Ball
The Bear
The Blue Boar
The Dog
The Fox
The Glovers Arms
The Masons Arms
The Orange Tree

The Queen's Own
The Rook's Nest
The Royal Oak
The Spider's Web
The Star
The Swan
The White Horse

Most people will remember where *The Marlborough* was. Perhaps there were other hostelries of which the Editor is ignorant. Any information would be of great assistance.

Historical comments

Some statements in the Historical Section have been questioned. It often occurs that people are talking about events in different times. Charlbury has a long history and local memories often go back to different periods.

Notices
Unsightly nuisance?

The Chairman of the Town Council approached the Editor and asked if he might put into this issue a letter about notices which appear in the town, pinned to telegraph poles. Some attention must be drawn to these features of our town.

Persons wishing to advertise events very often do not remove the notices after the event has taken place. Thus those of us who go for a morning walk use our initiative and remove them, but there are vandals who pluck at the notices and leave them hanging from a single pin.

There might be some consideration of the possibility of more noticeboards being put up in the town.

Litter

Litter remains a problem in the area of the public lavatories at the Spendlove Centre and on the play region of the Nine Acres Recreation Ground. On the morning of 30 May the Editor picked up 21 beer or Coca Cola cans and three bottles. And who overturned the rubbish bin at the top of the ground?

Police report
by PC Andy Sharples
PAPER SIFTING

I had started my summer round of cycling proficiency at Charlbury School and was handing out leaflets on crash helmets, when one boy said 'Can I have one?'

I replied 'But you have one already.' To that he replied 'Yes, but I want it for my gerbils to chew.' Bless him!

CONSTABULARY HEADQUARTERS

Charlbury Police Office is unfortunately what it states it is, an office, not a Police Station. It is therefore not manned. If I am in and not indisposed, on duty or off duty I will assist, if I can. I am unable to take production of vehicle documents, because it is not a Police Station. I have left a pad by the door, if you wish to leave me messages.

Street signs

Some review of street signs is needed. Drivers coming up Church Street sometimes do not know where Market Street is because the sign is on the east side of *The Rose & Crown*, where it is not immediately visible.

Another improvement might be the replacement of the broken sign directing drivers to Hixet Wood. All it shows at the moment is the letter H, the remainder of the sign having been broken off by a van negotiating the corner too closely when there was a traffic jam.

Charlbury diary, AD 1994
Recognition?

NOT *the Charlbury News Letter, Edition No. 2* appeared recently, stating that it was looking at '*Whats Wrong With Charlbury?*' It contained however an apology for the copy of the first edition which was put through my door with unpleasant words on it. The apology ended with the words: <u>Carry on Prof</u>. That article was followed by another which cast doubt on the Hard Surface Appeal which is a project of the Town Council. It said that there were more important things to consider, such as the play area on Nine Acres Recreation Ground. It asked: 'Is not a lot of money going to be spent on a small number of people?'

The project for the Hard Surface is an extension of the play area. It aims to provide facilities for people who are older than the juniors who use the play area. It also means to provide facilities, such as tennis, for women. It could provide an area in which the youth of the town, who at present gather in the evenings around the public lavatory at the Spendlove Centre, might engage in activities more harmless than drinking beer and smoking cigarettes.

The Editor of NOT *the Charlbury News Letter* might do us the service of disclosing his identity.

Open mouths and open minds

On 5 June 1994 a party of German visitors went into *The Rose & Crown* for a drink of beer. This matter has no significance except that, without any prompting, they opted for Archers *D-Day Special*. It would be wrong, however, to suggest that this was another Allied victory.

News in the Press
Shortage

Charlbury does not appear in the local press very much. Most of the reports in the *OXFORD MAIL* or *WITNEY GAZETTE* seem to be about the money which local townspeople have raised for good causes. In short, one can quote the Chinese saying that 'No news is good news.' In short, there is not much crime to report. Charlbury on the whole seems to be a peaceful place.

Charlbury pub crawls

If you live in Church Street you could almost literally have a pub crawl, were it not for the fact that there is a traffic problem. A visit to a pub is a means of acquiring information. *The Rose & Crown* is a useful place which provides a *terminus ad quem* for the councillors after a meeting on a Wednesday. *The Bell Hotel* brings us into contact with the world at large. Recently there have been visitors from Las Vegas, Los Angeles and even from British Columbia. A pub crawl, or equivalent, is these days a 'conversation crawl' which may be very interesting indeed. Alas! CHARLBURY NEWS cannot extend its coverage to world affairs. Thus caution is needed and all local information must be checked. A Charlbury rumour, which may start at the Co-Op, is often unrecognizable by the time it gets to the Post Office. Thus the Editor of CHARLBURY NEWS is warned by his wife not to give too much credence to what he hears!

Editorial
Finance

As usual thanks must be given to those who have made voluntary donations toward the publication costs of CHARLBURY NEWS. Mollie Crane ran a coffee morning which raised £50. Without this contribution the Editor would have been in a sorry state.

Going to press

The aim was to bring out a Midsummer Edition on or about 1 July. There was not much news in Charlbury. Everything seemed to be very peaceful and there were no major problems in the town. One problem is always that there are many activities which are to take place on or about the time *CHARLBURY NEWS* is going to press. It is therefore difficult to give a report on them. The only comfort came from a lady on the Woodstock Road, who said that but for *CHARLBURY NEWS* she would not know what was going on in the town. The Editor himself feels a bit isolated in the sense that he lives in Church Street. The majority of the population no longer lives in the centre of the old town. The danger is that important news from the fringes may be missed.

Charlbury people
J.E. Clifton

Jim Clifton had the misfortune to suffer an accident when he was doing a job at *The Bell Hotel*. A rung of the ladder on which he was standing gave way and he fell eight feet to the ground and broke his left ankle. Thus, if you see him with plaster on his left leg, you will know what has happened.

Father Robert Bulbeck

Father Bulbeck reached his 80th birthday on Monday, 16 May. A party was arranged for him in the Cornbury Room of *The Bell Hotel*. There was a call for those present to sing 'Happy birthday to you'. This was done with great glee. The Cornbury Room was filled with people, not all of them Catholics, which is an indication of the respect with which he is held in the town. A subscription was raised to buy him a new suit! Among the tributes paid to him was one by Canon Martin Chadwick, who said that Father Bulbeck decided to become a Jesuit rather than a Benedictine monk, which was the reason why he was with us today.

Charlbury Appraisal
Will it take place?

In the last issue of CHARLBURY NEWS it was stated that the Town Council was to initiate a Community Appraisal of our town in order to assess what improvements might be made. As far as the Editor knows there has been no discussion of what form the Appraisal will take.

There should be some analysis of the population. We can say definitely that it is highly literate.

Evidence of this is found in the large number of societies in the town. This indicates a strong intellectual interest in social problems. There is also strong cultural interest in the arts. A society as highly developed as Charlbury should not fail to present itself to the local government authorities.

There is a tendency to think of Charlbury as a rural haven of refuge, when in fact it is a town of growing importance. Let us hope that the Appraisal goes ahead as quickly as possible.

Warm weather

At the end of June the weather in Charlbury was very hot. At times it was over 85° in the shade. In fact, many of us had to shed our jackets. One Charlbury person escaped from the heat. That was Judith Scott of the Amber Lane Press who had taken a holiday in Finland in the area nearest to the Arctic Circle. She did not come back in time for a report of her holiday to be printed in this issue.

Latest news

NO NEWS AVAILABLE ON 30 JUNE.

Charlbury News
Street Fair stall

There will be a Street Fair stall for *Charlbury News* more or less outside the Editor's house next to the butcher's shop. Will readers who have suggestions please contact the Editor there?

It would help if they could write down beforehand any suggestions which are of some length. There will be a small bric-à-brac sale. Please support it if you can. Every penny counts these days!

Charlbury diary, AD 1994
Amber Lane Press
BOOKS ON THE THEATRE

The Amber Lane Press adjacent to *The Rose & Crown* does not excite much interest in the town. On the morning of 31 August, however, a very large wagon drew up on the bus stop. Miss Judith Scott said that it was delivering 9,000 reprints of one of the Amber Lane Press's publications. Thus what seems a very quiet business is very much more active than it would appear.

Axing of tree

On the wall of *The Rose & Crown* there was growing

a Buddleia, so called after the early 18th century botanist, Adam Buddle, but this has been cut down by workers of the local authority. Certainly Tom Page, the licensee of *The Rose & Crown*, did not ask for its removal. It grew long clusters, mauve in colour. Certainly the tree was a bit of a nuisance because it obscured the traffic coming up Church Street. It also accumulated rubbish underneath it, but it was not an eyesore. If it had been properly pruned it might have remained as an asset to Church Street.

Charlbury people
John Padbury

It was reported in the *OXFORD MAIL* that John Padbury of Yarnton has taken over as the new station master at Charlbury. He was the National Arts Awards Tap Dancing Champion seven times in the 1950s and 1960s. Padbury is an old Charlbury name, there being Padburies buried in the churchyard near the Church Lane gate.

Christmas celebration

We wish each other good cheer for Christmas and the New Year, but we must remember what our holidays mean. We have a long period of rest and relaxation. No doubt we will note that Christmas Day is when we see that the days are getting longer. This will remind us that our gardens will need attention. Many of us will therefore begin to dig over our gardens and prepare for early plantings. But we must remember that there are people in the town who perhaps have no families to visit them or for them to visit. They may have no gardens of which to think. Readers should think of what their neighbours are doing and, if they think that perhaps they are lonely, visit them to break up their period of isolation.

Stuart Ross

Mr Ross reports that he has decided not to move out of Charlbury, but will after all stay in the town.

Charlbury diary, AD 1994
Pessimism

One definition of a pessimist is that he looks both ways in a one-way street. This was in fact necessary recently when resurfacing took place at the junction of Thames Street, Dyers Hill and Market Street. Happily these problems were of short duration and we could be more optimistic relatively early on the Sunday after the road work finished.

CHARLBURY NEWS
Its future?
R.F. LESLIE

I began *CHARLBURY NEWS* at the suggestion of Father Robert Bulbeck in September 1990. It is comforting to know that many people in Charlbury like to read it, but the time has come to consider its future. I as Editor am beginning to suffer from a fatal disease, namely Old Age.

I therefore say to myself, in my capacity as Professor R.F. Leslie, BA, PhD, FRHS, Officer's Cross of the Order of Polonia Restituta, Médaille d'Honneur de la Société Européenne de Culture, formerly 164709 Captain R.F. Leslie, Royal Armoured Corps, served 1939–46, wounded, Mentioned in Despatches, that I can no longer be as active as I was.

One of my activities which I might cut down on is the editorship of *CHARLBURY NEWS*. One of these days there will be a loud clang in Church Street when I kick the bucket. The danger is that *CHARLBURY NEWS* will disappear even before that event.

Charlbury personality
Freddie Jones

One of Charlbury's personalities is the actor, Freddie Jones, of Crinan House, Market Street. Freddie visits *The Bell Hotel* from time to time for a drink and a chat. Recently he visited us all in our homes, playing a part in *Just William* on television. He was the neatly dressed Sir Giles who was very kind to William. On television Freddie was rather noisier than he normally is in *The Bell*! People do not recognize him when he is pointed out to them there. Let us hope he continues to appear on television so that visitors can identify him without having to be told who he is.

Charlbury pubs
Conversation centres

One of the pleasing features of our town is the fact that we can go for a drink with no intention of getting drunk. There are people from Chadlington who come here merely for a talk. Let us hope Charlbury maintains its reputation in this respect.

W.D. Campbell
(3 November 1905–23 November 1994)

We had noted that Bill Campbell's articles, entitled

The Country Diary on Wednesday in the *Guardian*, were complicated by his illness, but on 23 November his article appeared as normal, as if he had written it himself. We were surprised therefore to hear later in the day that he had died that very morning on his home, Ticknell Corner on The Slade.

Bill was the son of the head gardener in Cornbury Park and worked in Charlbury as a teacher, in fact in the school where he was himself educated. There are many people in the town who were taught by him. Our respect for him means that he had written his own obituary in his lifetime.

Latest news
Vandalism

23 December: A window of the public convenience at the Spendlove Centre car park was smashed overnight. Someone removed the paving stones on the wall at the corner opposite the public conveniences. Who are these vandals? One suggestion is that they are not Charlbury people, but louts who come into the town from adjacent places. They seem to be attracted by the kebab van which sells food there by night.

1995 and all that
What sort of a year will it be?

We were told that the Gifford Trust was proposing to sell the section of the Playing Close upon which the Community Education Centre is built, the former British School, founded in 1815. The project was for a sheltered housing scheme to accommodate elderly persons.

The scheme was provisional and there were some misgivings locally. Then rumours began to circulate. It was said that Hartwell Properties Ltd, who had acquired the Spendlove Centre, were prepared to offer vacant land on the Spendlove site for the construction of a Community Centre building. Thus a meeting was called for Friday, 17 February for the matter to be discussed by the community. The situation bore a close resemblance to the famous work, *1066 And All That*. Nothing was certain for the time being.

Vandalism
Who is responsible?

It is learned that the kebab van is no longer operating in Charlbury because damage was done to its tyres and the proprietors have taken it elsewhere. Damage has been done also to the equipment on

Nine Acres. The picnic tables had their tops ripped off. The vandals were equally destructive of the Tarzan Trail. Evidently part of it was vandalized with the help of a chain saw. Certainly no one could have broken a plank of wood at least four inches thick with his bare hands.

Quite clearly the vandals are suffering from a severe mental disorder. What pleasure can they get out of their misconduct? No normal person would find anything pleasing in mindless destruction. It is a saying that the wisest memories we have are the tomfool things we do when we are young. Perhaps these offenders should reflect now on their deeds and convert them into wise memories now.

Good Food Shop

The Good Food Shop in Sheep Street reports that it is now selling varieties of fish including kippers, smoked salmon and smoked mackerel. Many people are buying sandwiches and cake for lunch. The shop now sells a wider variety of cakes than it has done previously.

Charlbury diary, AD 1995
Youth Hostel

Charlbury is not a metropolis, but some of the

visitors to the Youth Hostel give it an international flavour. Recently 32 Americans from Colorado stayed there on their way from Stratford-on-Avon to Oxford. Later in the summer a cricket team is coming from Soweto in South Africa. It is making its first tour of the United Kingdom. Doubtless we should give its members a warm welcome if they appear in the town, but as yet there is no guarantee that they will examine us in our native habitat.

Street Fayre

We note that the Street Fair is now described by its organizing committee as the 'Fayre', which presumably is a medieval spelling for such an occasion. Perhaps the organizers of the Fair might go the whole hog and use one of the older spellings of Charlbury. It is said in Adrian Room's *Dictionary of Place-Names in the United Kingdom* (1988) that the spelling of 'Charlbury' in about AD 1000 was recorded as *Ceorlingburh* meaning 'the fortified place of Ceorl's people'. To this we might add the spelling of the definite article with the use of the thorn, the Old English and Old Norse letter for *th*. Thus we could have on the great day '*Ye Ceorlingburh Straet Fayre*'.

Apparently the word *fair* is not of English origin,

but is derived from the Old French word *feire*. Thus perhaps the word *fayre* can be used, but it apparently does not appear in modern English dictionaries.

Charlbury gossip

It is said that once a rumour starts at the Co-Op it becomes unrecognizable by the time it gets to the Post Office, but a recent example makes that statement seem only a slight truth. A Charlbury resident recently won a small prize on the State Lottery, but the figure was enlarged into £250,000 in a short time. He is now congratulated with broad grins by people whom he does not know.

Charlbury pubs
Only four left

In the 19th century there were nine pubs licensed in Charlbury, and until recently there were still six. Alas, today there are only four. In the old days Charlbury was a market town and on market days there was always plenty of trade. Many of the licensees had other occupations to occupy them when there was no market. Thus Mr Harris at *The Bull* was a carpenter and Mr Constable at *The Bell* was a plumber.

More important perhaps is the fact that the social structure of life has changed. In the old days families were larger and fathers got out of the house when mother was putting the children to bed.

English pubs are institutions. My knowledge of East Europeans is that they dislike drinking in bars, because they are places of drunkenness, but they admire English pubs because conversation is more important than drink. A Pole once said to me on entering a pub 'Is this some sort of club?'

Let us hope therefore that our pubs will maintain their present social atmosphere and stay social centres where opinions can be exchanged and news circulated. I was attracted to come and live in Charlbury because I stayed at weekends in *The Bell* and liked the people I met.

Good Food Shop
Sheep Street

This shop has a wide variety of foods, cereals, pulses and pastas.

It is supplied with fresh bread daily and has a large stock of English and Continental cheeses, quiches and many other, locally cooked goodies.

PLEASE TRY IT.

Latest
Vandalism
NINE ACRES PLAY EQUIPMENT

It is now considered that the swing plank of the Tarzan Trail was broken as a result of natural causes and the makers are to replace it.

Playground of school

The *OXFORD TIMES* (31 March 1995) reported that the Oxfordshire County Council agreed 'in principle' to sell the playground of the old Primary School to Beechcroft for the building of sheltered housing, subject to conditions which will ensure the quality of a new community education building.

(The above report is said to be totally incorrect.)

Further vandalism
Sheep Street

On the night of 19 July 1995 there was vandalism in so far as a thief took off the doorhandle of the Good Food Shop in an attempt to break into it. There are some doubts about his sobriety. He was also sick all over the door. This would seem to indicate that he is of local origin because someone coming into town from a distance would not have drunk so much alcohol to be as drunk as that, if he were to go home by car.

Charlbury diary, AD 1995
Bull at Charlbury

Mr Flynn has removed the notice on the Sheep Street side of *The Bull*, which said THE BULL AT CHARLBURY. The Editor suggested to him that you could no longer get a reading on the oxometer as you walked past *The Bull*. Mr Flynn knew that was an instrument for measuring the amount of bull in any project.

Good Food Shop
OPENING HOURS

The Good Food Shop is now opening from 9 a.m. to 5 p.m. on Mondays to Fridays and from 9 a.m. to 12.30 p.m. on Saturdays. This is a great improvement and means that we do not have to do our timing as carefully when we go down Sheep Street.

News gathering

Getting information is the most difficult task of the Editor. Many people ask for the final date for submission, but they ignore the fact that the Editor must have sufficient time to type his articles. My standard reply to people asking for a date is 'Do it now as the actress said to the bishop!' This seems rather naughty, but it is necessary.

1995 and afterwards
What will happen to Charlbury?

Between now and AD 2000 much is scheduled to take place. The future of the old Primary School and the Spendlove Centre will be decided. It will be possible to develop the present site of the Spendlove Centre. The disappearance of that building will not be a great loss. It never did harmonize with the other buildings in the historic centre of the town. The real question is what will be put in its place.

Charlbury news
Shortage

Once upon a time when Suzanne Huband and her husband visited Charlbury for a drink in *The White Hart* there was a bit more news in our local press than there is now, but we have had some information in the *OXFORD MAIL* on 24 November. It was reported that 3½ tonnes of Cotswold stone was stolen at Banbury Hill Farm. How anyone can have had a customer for that amount of stone is difficult to imagine, but it disappeared while the workmen were having their lunch. A children's yellow go-cart was taken from a garden in Hughes Close. Who the thieves are it cannot be said, but it would appear that they do not live in the town, but come in from outside.

Charlbury guide
Rough instruction

People want to know how to identify old buildings in Charlbury. They take visitors around the older section of the town which is clearly of historic interest. They cannot put a date to some of the older buildings, for which reason a rough guide may be of use.

One of the best guides is the map of Charlbury drawn up in AD 1761, when the Duke of Marlborough acquired Walcot from the Jenkinson family. Robert Banks Jenkinson (1770–1825), the second Lord Liverpool, was the longest serving Prime Minister in the United Kingdom. This map shows how the historic town consisted of Church Street, Church Lane, Market Street, Thames Street, Park Street and Sheep Street, with Hixet Wood as a settlement on the fringe.

One quick means of establishing the date of a building is the size of the window panes. The smaller the pane the earlier its origin. Very small window panes indicate existence as early as the 16th century. Within a house a circular staircase has an origin dating between 1620 and 1640 AD. A staircase in *The Bull* is clearly of that origin. A fireplace with a curved wooden arch is said to indicate an origin of before AD 1700. At one time there must have been such an arch in *The Bell* because there are signs of its having been cut off.

Another means of learning more about buildings is to consult the writings of John Kibble, the stonemason, who among other things constructed the monument on the Playing Close. Kibble's works tend to be gossipy and roam all over the district. Nevertheless, they lack the detail needed for more definite information.

Charlbury diary, AD 1995
Ideal barmaid?

The Editor drew the attention of the licensees of *The Bull Inn* to the celebrated limerick on the subject of a barmaid in Sale, Cheshire:

> On the breasts of a Barmaid in Sale
> Are tattooed all the prices of ale
> And across her behind
> For the sake of the blind
> Is the same information in Braille.

It does not appear that Roy and Suzanne Flynn will apply similar standards to the bar in *The Bull*.

Kenneth Cotton

Kenneth Cotton (baptized Hubert) of Market Street is one of the oldest inhabitants of Charlbury. He is 93 years old, but he is active enough to get out in the morning to do his drinking. He goes to *The Rose & Crown* where he drinks his half pint of bitter. The fact that he goes out for his morning walk is a good sign and shows that he is still a member of the community. Let us hope that he goes on to achieve a hundred years and can still go out for his half pint!

Alphabet
Cockney version

In the Editor's young days there was a standard Cockney analysis of the alphabet. Is there any corresponding local equivalent? Are there any local limericks apart from 'There was a Young Lady of Wantage'? Is there anything similar that can be put down as part of a local tradition of folklore? If so, will anyone who remembers it put it down on paper? We will print it as part of the local tradition.

Our policeman
Report

Paul Girling has recently taken up his duties as our policeman in Charlbury. He is 28 years of age and married to Tracy who was born and bred in Chipping Norton. They have a German shepherd dog called Clint.

He considers himself to be one of the luckiest men alive to be posted to what he considers one of the most beautiful parts of the country. He finds the people warm and friendly.

He says the residents of Charlbury need not worry about a new policeman. He thinks most people are law-abiding, but asks you not to think he has a soft touch. Anyone caught breaking the law will be dealt with fairly and firmly.

He says you can go and talk to him at any time. If he is not in the police office, you can use the message pad outside and he will get in touch with you as soon as he can.

Charlbury diary, AD 1996
Street light
CHURCH STREET

On 11 June workmen arrived to repair the street lamp on the north side of Church Street. Let us hope that it is not left to lie idle for so long again.

Local guide
Places in the area

A guide to the local area, if you want to know about it, is *The Hidden Places of the Thames & Chilterns* (edited by Shane Scott). Chapter 4, 'The heart of Oxfordshire', does not include Charlbury. (This book is on sale at News & Things at a reduced price.)

Charlbury gossip
Fact and fiction?

Rumours circulate in Charlbury. A rumour which is mentioned in Church Street, repeated in Market Street and discussed in Sheep Street, becomes a broad approximation to the truth in the course of a few days.

It has been said that *The Bull Inn* is up for sale, but Roy Flynn, the licensee and owner, says that this is not true as far as he knows. Equally he says that it is not true that he is going to buy *The Rose & Crown*.

Thus we must not believe all the stories we hear. One of the purposes of *CHARLBURY NEWS* is to put rumours on a firm foundation.

Wesley Barrell
Conversion of site

One of the tragedies of Charlbury is that the furniture firm, Wesley Barrell, is to close. Permission has been given to convert the site of the factory into a housing estate. It was in the old days a brewery, when there were no less than six malthouses in the town. It then became a wool staple.

The tendency in Charlbury is for professional firms to move into the town. On the other hand there are fewer facilities for the inhabitants. The Town Council should turn its attention to what is becoming a nuisance. If Wesley Barrell's premises are going to provide an area for housing development, we need more shops.

Coffeehouse meeting
Visit of Bishop of Oxford

The Coffeehouse was filled to overflowing on the morning of 8 June, when the Bishop of Oxford, the Rt Rev. Richard Harries, visited the town to discuss a work of the Rev. Donald Reeves, the co-owner of the Coffeehouse.

This work is entitled *Down to Earth—New Vision of the Church*. Donald Reeves conceives the Church of England as having a part to play in all the problems which face us in the modern epoch. Let us hope that the Rev. Donald Reeves will arrange further meetings in Charlbury, but we must say with regret that the Coffeehouse is too small for such interesting occasions.

New vicar

It was announced in St Mary's Church on 22 September that the new vicar will be the Rev. Judith French, at present a curate near Rugby. This is a new venture for Charlbury. For the first time the vicar will be a woman. This announcement was received with much pleasure in the town, especially among the women. Let us hope that the Rev. Judith French will enjoy being here in the town. Let us hope that she blends with it as much as Canon Martin Chadwick did, and that we will meet her in the town for the occasional chat as we did with Martin Chadwick.

Margery Leslie, OBE
1917–1996

As was generally reported in the national and local press, Margery Leslie died on 6 August. She had a wide and varied career and retired from the post of Principal of the Richmond Adult College, Richmond-on-Thames, where she was awarded the OBE for her efforts.

I was convinced that Charlbury would be a place where she could engage in the problems of local life. We bought the house which is now called Market House in Church Street as a home of retirement and she quickly blended with the community, serving on various committees, including what was then the Parish Council. She was greatly interested in the Nine Acres Recreation Ground and took charge of raising money for the construction of the hard play surface, which is now known as THE MARGERY LESLIE COURTS, a tribute to the effort she put into the work of collecting the money for what is now a social centre of the town.

Charlbury weather

One local wit said that we have been having Tory weather, because it has been wet and windy. Whether or not his comment is correct, we leave that open to the readership. It is a relief to have had the rain. Some of us who are gardeners have thought that we have not had enough rain in recent months.

Equally we have been short of sunshine during the flowering of our apple trees. Some of them did not produce any fruit at all, presumably because wasps and bees found it too cold to get out and about in the spring. Let us hope that next year will be better.

Royal British Legion
Women's section

Disturbing reports appeared in the *OXFORD MAIL*, the *WITNEY GAZETTE* and the *OXFORD TIMES* concerning Miss Freda Lidgey. It was reported that £3,000 was missing from the funds of two branches of the women's sections of the Royal British Legion in Charlbury and Oxford. It was reported that Miss Freda Lidgey of Jeffs Terrace was arrested and cautioned by the police.

The reports were extremely vague, but this has not prevented gossip from circulating in the town. Miss Lidgey has apparently resigned from both her posts and is therefore no longer involved in this work. It would be unwise to repeat casual gossip current in the town. The printed articles are too vague to justify that.

Traffic trauma
Meeting, 22 November

The Council for the Protection of Rural England (Chipping Norton–Woodstock area) held a well-attended meeting in the Memorial Hall to discuss rural roads in Oxfordshire. While we may agree with the general principles they set out, there was no discussion of the problems we face every day in Charlbury.

If you wish to cross the street from *The Bull* to the Library you have to be very careful lest you be knocked down by a car. In Market Street you may be struck by a larger vehicle. Thames Street is very narrow and there is a danger that you may be hit when two vehicles are passing one another.

Charlbury has its problems as well as Oxfordshire as a whole. A meeting to discuss them would be welcome.

Charlbury diary, AD 1996
Charlbury occupied

Charlbury was occupied for a whole week by a television team of the BBC, which was filming for the drama, *Dalziel & Pascoe*. One of the most serious inconveniences for drinkers was that *The Bell Hotel* was closed for the whole morning and early afternoon of Tuesday, 15 October. No doubt we will enjoy watching the result on television, when we will discover what an exciting place Charlbury might be.

Seat in Church Street

The seat in Church Street outside *The Rose & Crown*, intended originally for people waiting for the buses on the north side of the street, was not usable because it was covered by birds' droppings. It has now been moved to lower down the street, where it will not be exposed so much to the birds' droppings. This move is much welcomed. It is moreover nearer the bus stop.

Autumn edition
Late production

I apologize for the lateness of this edition of

Charlbury News. This was due to the death of my wife, Mrs Margery Leslie, who died on 6 August. There have been all manner of problems to deal with and this has delayed my work. In future the editor will be Mrs Lynette Murphy of Hundley Cottage, Hundley Way.

I will continue to do what I can to help her. Living in Church Street, I gather much information from passers-by and from the various hostelries almost adjacent to my home. Mrs Murphy will need as much information as she can get from Charlbury organizations and clubs. She says that the new *Charlbury News* will represent her personality and not mine. Perhaps that will see a great improvement in its presentation. I therefore say farewell to the people of Charlbury and wish them well for the future.

Two-minute silence

There have been objections to the demand for a two-minute silence on 11 November. The Remembrance Day march seems to recall the achievements of our forces during the wars, but not the sufferings we endured.

I was serving with the 15th/19th King's Royal Hussars, a reconnaissance regiment, when I was wounded on 2 April 1945. We were outflanking the Germans near Osnabruck and I discovered a bridge which was not occupied. I crossed over it and got to the top of the hill, thus opening the way for the division to advance. My tank fell into a fault in the land drainage. It could not move and I asked my co-driver to get out on the blind side and put the tow-rope on. He was too frightened and I got out of the turret to do it myself. As I was lifting the tow-rope, I was hit in the leg by a bullet.

Then my troubles started. I was taken back from one casualty clearing station to another. I recall one occasion when I was left in a ward surrounded by wounded German prisoners of war. An orderly came round and said 'What are you doing here amid this scum, sir?' I was taken to an officers' ward and put on a stretcher in a corridor. I heard a nurse say: 'That officer in that room is dying.' The ward sister said: 'Get on with your job.' After a while the nurse said: 'That officer is dead, sister.' The ward sister said: 'Well, get him out of the bed and put someone else in it.' I then got a bed, but I was still dripping with blood.

When we observe the two-minute silence I recall these experiences. War is unpleasant. There is no glory in it for those of us who are killed, or were wounded.

Where to drink in Charlbury
Guide to the pubs

We may ask ourselves where we can drink in Charlbury. We have only four pubs left. In the old days there were nine licensed in Charlbury.

A visit to a local pub is determined by what you want to do. *The Rose & Crown* is mainly a place in which to have a drink. There is also a pool table. The younger generation can go for a game and not interrupt the more senior citizens. The pool table is removed from the main bar and exclamations of excitement are not heard to any extent in the main bar.

The Bell is still a hotel and attracts visitors from all over England. Thus *The Bell* has a national as well as local role.

The Bull Inn is not the great place for conversation as it was 20 years ago when it attracted many mature locals. You could look out into the streets and note who was passing by. If you did not know them there would be someone present who could give you a brief biography. On the other hand, the food at *The Bull* is good. If you have a distinguished visitor with a taste for good food, *The Bull* is a place to take him.

The Farmers Arms gives custom to people living

in Hixet Wood. I have not been to *The Farmers* for some time and cannot report on it accurately.

On the whole we must agree that our local pubs provide an excellent service and need to be patronized.

Freddie Jones
New role?

Freddie Jones normally appears in reviews of plays in which he has distinguished himself, but he now has achieved fame as a cook. The *OXFORD MAIL* on 5 November revealed that he has a recipe for Curried Fruit Bats, whatever they may be. You have to serve them with mango chutney, basmati rice and curried vegetables. Some of us would like to try the dish before cooking it ourselves.

Where is Charlbury?

If we ask one another where Charlbury is, we can expect to be told that it is the northern part of West Oxfordshire. This turns out to be a simple answer which does not answer national attitudes. For the purposes of the BBC we lie in the South East, but for ITV we are in the South Midlands. When it comes to weather forecasts, we turn out to be in Central

Southern England, the West Midlands, or the East Midlands according to the weather when it appears.

Another question is whether we are in the Cotswolds. In the old days some of the more ancient locals objected strongly to that conception on the grounds that they wanted nothing to do with Gloucestershire people. Today it seems to be generally accepted that we are in part of the Cotswolds. Any geographer will confirm that.

Latest news
Christmas is coming
WHAT'S NEW ABOUT THAT?

Christmas is a time when we relax, and we enjoy ourselves, irrespective of the problems we have in the rest of the year. For some people life is not like that. They spend Christmas Day by themselves, wondering what life will be like on Boxing Day. If there is a person like that living near you, pay him or her a visit and offer a drink or comfort. That will break the day up and make it seem less miserable.

Farewell message

I am giving up the editorship of *CHARLBURY NEWS*. This is not because I am tired of doing it, but simply because I am now 78 years old and have become very tottery. I need to take a walking stick with me these days lest I fall over in the street. I have done that once and I have done it indoors.

I am not the originator of *CHARLBURY NEWS*. The idea was conceived by Father Robert Bulbeck, who induced me to compose it. I hope that the reproduction of Charlbury gossip in a literary form has appealed to the inhabitants of the town.

I am not retiring from Charlbury. I will continue to live here. After all, I live next door to *The Bell*. We used to stay there in the old days and came to like the town, for which reason we retired here. Opposite is *The Rose & Crown* and up the street is *The Bull*. These are good places for conversation. Alas! owing to the traffic trauma I cannot exactly have a pub crawl. Doubtless I will continue to have a drink and make some contribution to the new *CHARLBURY NEWS*, but I may in the course of time have to sell up and move either into an old people's home, or to live with my daughter in London. I thank the people of Charlbury for the friendship they have shown me over the years.

Farewell word game

How many words of FOUR letters or more can you

track down in this Farewell Word Game? At least one will have NINE letters and all must contain the central letter. Use each letter only once.

> RHA
> LUR
> BCY

EDITOR: PROFESSOR R.F. LESLIE
Market House, Church Street,
Charlbury, OX7 3PP

The following four-letter words can be made from the letters: blur, burl, CHARLBURY, chub, churl, club, curl, curly, curry, haul, hurl, hurly, hurry, lubra, ruby, rural.
If there are more, please let us know.

R.F. Leslie
1918–2002

GEOFFREY WALTON PRACTICE

Mining Geologists and Geotechnical Engineers
Mine and Quarry Designers

We are most grateful for Professor Leslie's assistance with social contacts that led to our working for Belchatow Lignite Mine in Western Poland.

Robert—your trenchant views are much missed by
the 'man in the Rose and Crown'.

Upton House, Market Street, Charlbury, Oxford, OX7 3PJ
Tel.: 01608 810374   Fax: 01608 810093   gwp@gwalton.co.uk

Co-op Community dividend scheme*

A minimum of 1% of the Society's profits are returned to projects to benefit the local community through the Community Dividend Scheme.

If you think a project you know of could qualify for a grant of up to £1,000

call 01865 256235
for more information

Oxford, Swindon & Gloucester

The Bell at Charlbury

1700

'The Bell Hotel brings us into contact with the world at large.'
R.F. Leslie

À la carte restaurant
Bar meals
Conference facilities
Real log fires
Live music every month

Martin Lyall
Church Street, Charlbury, Oxfordshire OX7 3PP
Telephone: 01608 810278 Fax: 01608 811447
Email: reservationsatthebell@msn.com
Web: www.bellhotel-charlbury.co.uk

VINCENT PHARMACY

Market Street, Charlbury

01608 810315

We are pleased to be able to support the Charlbury Community Centre Appeal through the sale of this book. The Pharmacy has been in town, at this site in Market Street, since the early 1900s. Professor Leslie was a regular—almost daily—visitor during his years in Charlbury, purchasing his needs while gathering the town's news and gossip.

OPEN ALL DAY
MONDAY TO FRIDAY 9 a.m.–6 p.m.
SATURDAY 9 a.m.–1 p.m

CHARLBURY POST OFFICE

for

CAR TAX
TRAVEL INSURANCE
CURRENCY (no charge)
BANKING (Co-Op • Barclays • Lloyds/TSB)
HANKO MACHINE

You can also bring us your letters and parcels, your utilities bills . . . and even your gossip!

Handmade - exclusively to your order.

WESLEY-BARRELL

3 Bridge Street Witney

For our brochures and enquiries phone 01993 776682

www.wesley-barrell.co.uk

design classics

THE CHARLBURY BREWING COMPANY LIMITED

Tel.: 01608 811522 / 079790 97 544

Resident chef: Mr Dan Oliver

The business was started in 1875 by my great-grandfather, James Edwards, as a pub, brewery and carriage business.

I left our last business, *The Red Lion*, Kings Mills, Wrexham in 1984 and came to Charlbury. On 21 May 2004 we opened at *The Farmers*, Charlbury. This was originally named *The Three Horseshoes* but the name was changed to *The Railway* in 1852, when construction workers on the Worcester line walked to the pub for their lunch. It was changed to *The Farmers* in the late 1980s, but we decided to change it back to its original name.

My wife, Sally-Anne, was laboratory manager at Morrell's of Oxford for 11 years and she will be brewing approximately three real ales from organic products. The chef produces good wholesome food cooked on the premises.

The pub is 'family friendly' (we have four youngsters of our own!) We look forward to meeting new friends and you can be sure of a friendly (and changing) environment. Thanks to all our friends in Charlbury for their support.

Director: Barry Dodman-Edwards MBA BSc CEng MICE
Company Secretary: Sally-Anne Dodman-Edwards MIOSH

The Bull Inn

Sheep Street
Charlbury
Oxfordshire OX7 3RR
Tel.: 01608 810689

The Bull Inn is a privately owned 16th century coaching house situated in the centre of Charlbury. It prides itself on home-cooked food using local produce where possible. It has a restaurant seating forty people and a bar accommodating a further thirty. The restaurant can be booked for private parties and other functions.

We also have four *en suite* rooms, all with tea-making facilities, bottled water, TVs and DVD players.

'If you have a distinguished visitor with a taste for good food, *The Bull* is a place to take him.' *Professor Robert Leslie.*

THE ROSE & CROWN
CHARLBURY

MARKET STREET, CHARLBURY
Tel: 01608 810103

Email: thomas.topbeerpub@tiscali.co.uk

The Traditional Pub with the emphasis on **BEER**

"The *Rose & Crown* is mainly a place in which to have a drink."
– *R. F. Leslie*

**CAMRA North Oxon Branch
PUB OF THE YEAR in both
2002 and 2003**

THE GOOD FOOD SHOP

39 Sheep Street
Charlbury
Tel./fax 01608 811157

FINE FOODS
FRESHLY MADE SANDWICHES
BUFFET CATERING

'PLEASE TRY IT.'
(R.F. Leslie)

It was as long ago as 1995 that Professor Robert Leslie first reported on plans for a new Community Centre in Charlbury. Unfortunately, due to a series of poor decisions, the original plans ended in failure; but early in 2004 a new team stepped in to revive the project, and to provide some of the facilities that the town will need in the 21st century.

In order to succeed, it is crucial that the project receives the active support of as many people in the community as possible. For more information on how to help, please contact the appeal coordinator, Lynette Murphy (01608 810549), or Edward Fenton (01608 811196).